Impressum
Verlag: BABADADA GmbH, Nedderfeld 112 , 22529 Hamburg
Geschäftsführer / Verlagsleitung: Harald Hof
Druck: Books on Demand GmbH, In de Tarpen 42, 22848 Norderstedt

Imprint
Publisher: BABADADA GmbH, Nedderfeld 112 , 22529 Hamburg, Germany
Managing Director / Publishing direction: Harald Hof
Print: Books on Demand GmbH, In de Tarpen 42, 22848 Norderstedt

مدرسه

school

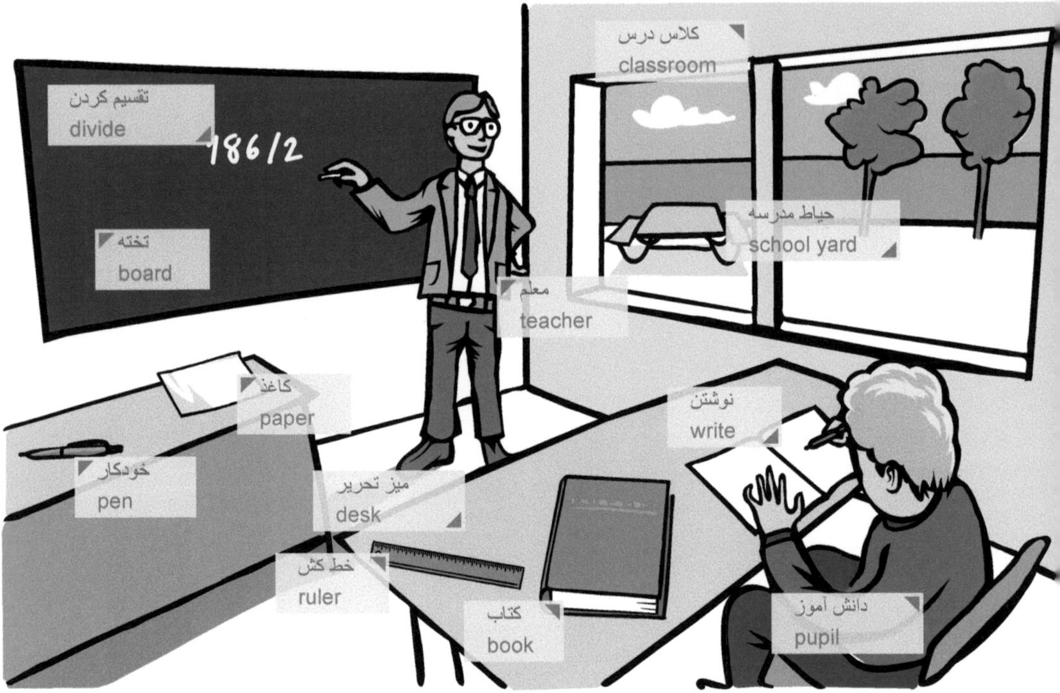

کلاس درس
classroom
تقسیم کردن
divide
186/2
حیاط مدرسه
school yard
تخته
board
معلم
teacher
کاغذ
paper
نوشتن
write
خودکار
pen
میز تحریر
desk
خط کش
ruler
کتاب
book
دانش آموز
pupil

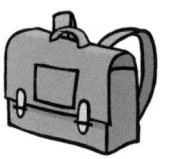

کیف مدرسه

satchel

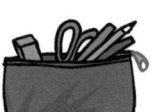

جامدادی

pencil case

مداد

pencil

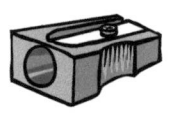

تراش

pencil sharpener

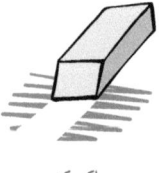

پاک کن

rubber

دفتر رسم

drawing pad

طراحی

drawing

قلم مو

paintbrush

جعبه ی آبرنگ

paint box

قیچی

scissors

چسب

glue

کتاب تمرین

exercise book

تکلیف خانه

homework

12

رقم

number

2+2

جمع کردن

add

5-2

تفریق کردن

subtract

2×2

ضرب کردن

multiply

محاسبه کردن

calculate

A

حرف الفبا

letter

ABCDEFG
HIJKLMN
OPQRSTU
VWXYZ

الفبا

alphabet

کلمه

word

متن

text

خواندن

read

گچ

chalk

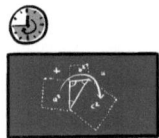

درس

lesson

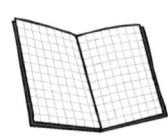

ثبت نام

register

امتحان

exam

مدرک رسمی

certificate

لباس مدرسه

school uniform

تحصیلات

education

دانشنامه

encyclopedia

دانشگاه

university

میکروسکوپ

microscope

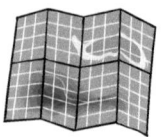

نقشه

map

سبد کاغذ باطله

waste-paper basket

سفر

travel

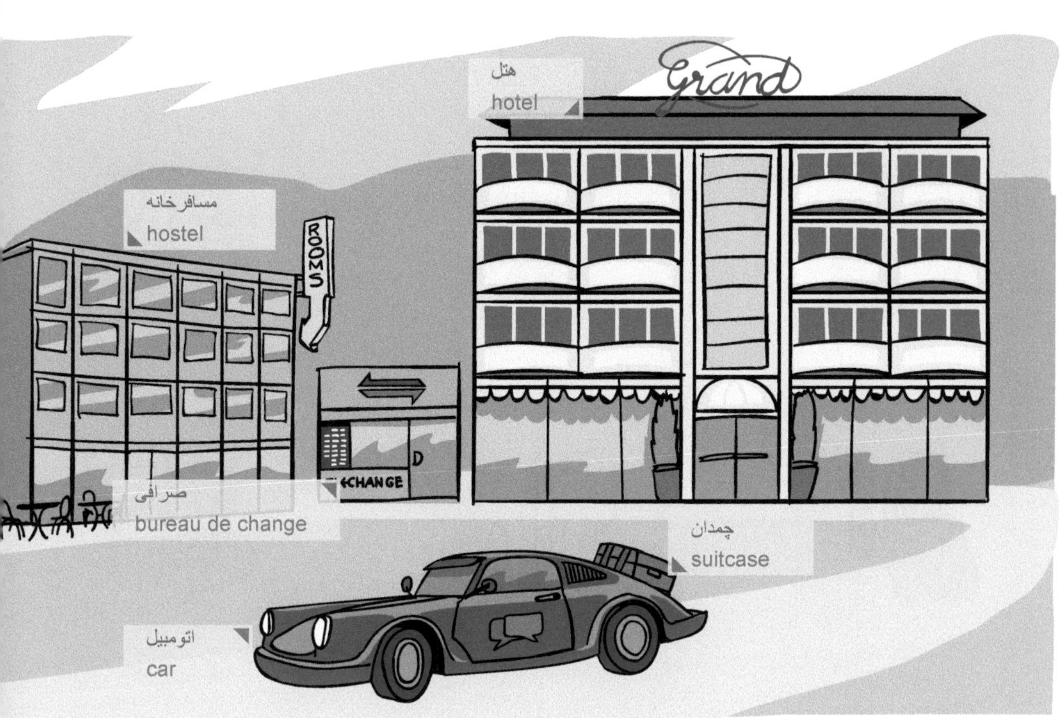

هتل
hotel
Grand
مسافرخانه
hostel
ROOMS
صرافی
bureau de change
چمدان
suitcase
اتومبیل
car

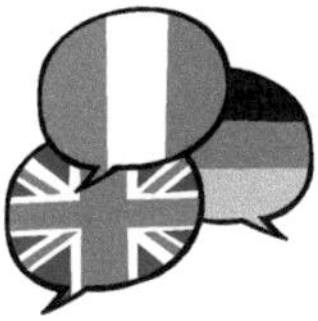

زبان

language

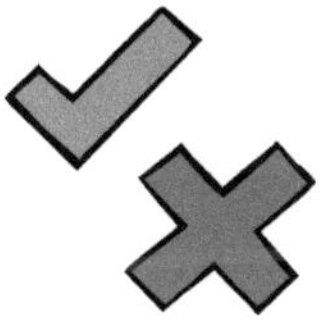

بله / خیر

yes / no

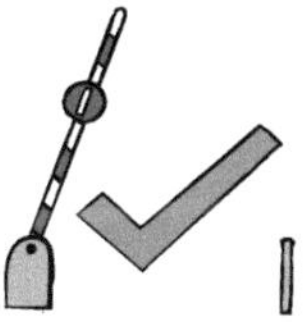

اُکی

Okay

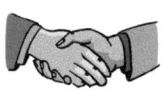

سلام

hello

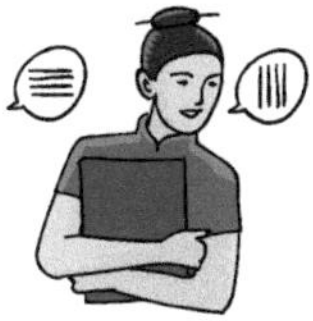

مترجم

translator

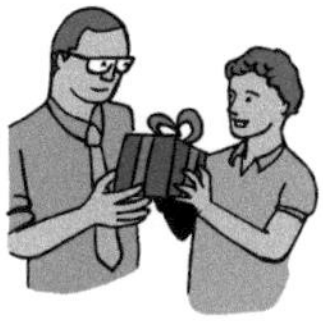

ممنون

Thank you

قیمت ... چه قدر است؟

how much is...?

من متوجه نمی شوم

I do not understand

مشکل

problem

عصر بخیر! / شب بخیر!

Good evening!

صبح بخیر!

Good morning!

شب بخیر!

Good night!

خدانگهدار

bye bye

جهت

direction

بار سفر

luggage

کیف

bag

کوله پشتی

backpack

مهمان

guest

اتاق

room

کیسه خواب

sleeping bag

خیمه

tent

مرکز راهنمای گردشگران
....
tourist information

ساحل
....
beach

کارت اعتباری
....
credit card

صبحانه
....
breakfast

نهار
....
lunch

شام
....
dinner

بلیط
....
ticket

آسانسور
....
lift

مهر
....
stamp

مرز
....
border

گمرک
....
customs

سفارتخانه
....
embassy

ویزا
....
visa

گذرنامه
....
passport

حمل و نقل
transport

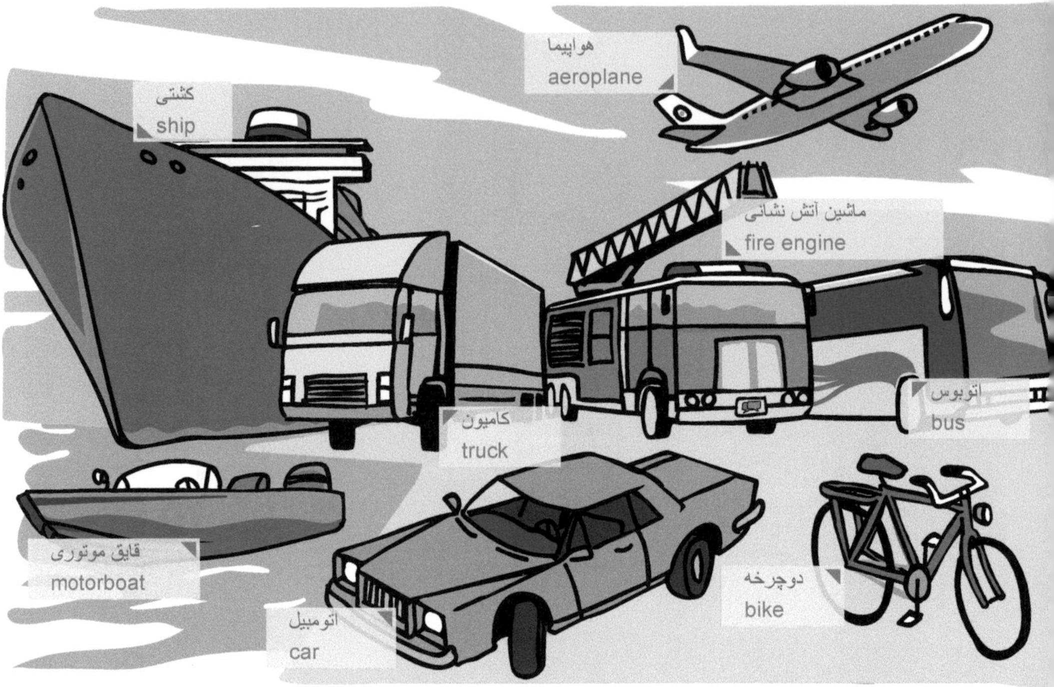

هواپیما
aeroplane
کشتی
ship
ماشین آتش نشانی
fire engine
اتوبوس
bus
کامیون
truck
قایق موتوری
motorboat
دوچرخه
bike
اتومبیل
car

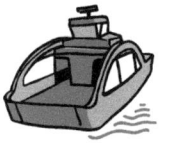

کشتی مسافربری
ferry

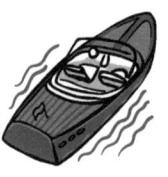

قایق
boat

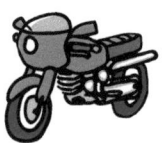

موتورسیکلت
motorbike

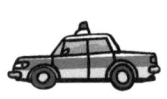

ماشین پلیس
police car

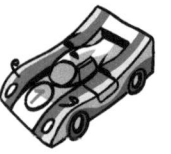

ماشین مسابقه
racing car

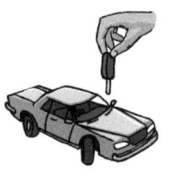

ماشین کرایه ای
rental car

به اشتراک گذاری اتوموبیل

car sharing

جرثقیل

breakdown truck

ماشین حمل زباله

refuse truck

موتور

motor

بنزین

fuel

پمپ بنزین

petrol station

تابلو راهنمایی و رانندگی

traffic sign

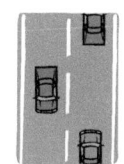

عبور و مرور

traffic

ترافیک

traffic jam

پارکینگ

car park

ایستگاه قطار

train station

ریل راه آهن

tracks

قطار

train

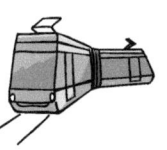

قطار برقی

tram

واگن

carriage

هلیکوپتر

helicopter

فرودگاه

airport

برج

tower

مسافر

passenger

کانتینر

container

کارتن

carton

گاری

cart

سبد

basket

به پرواز درآمدن / فرود آمدن

take off / land

شهر

city

دهکده

village

مرکز شهر

city centre

خانه

house

سینما
cinema

تبلیغ
advert

چراغ خیابان
street lamp

CINEMA

خیابان
street

تاکسی
taxi

دکه
snack shop

عابر پیاده
pedestrian

پیاده رو
pavement

خط کشی عابر پیاده
zebra crossing

سطل آشغال بزرگ
bin

چهارراه
crossing

چراغ راهنما
traffic lights

کلبه
....
hut

آپارتمان
....
flat

ایستگاه قطار
....
train station

ساختمان شهرداری
....
town hall

موزه
....
museum

مدرسه
....
school

دانشگاه

university

بانک

bank

بیمارستان

hospital

هتل

hotel

داروخانه

pharmacy

اداره

office

کتابفروشی

book shop

مغازه

shop

گل فروشی

florist's

سوپرمارکت

supermarket

بازار

market

فروشگاه بزرگ

department store

ماهی فروش

fishmonger's

مرکز خرید

shopping centre

بندر

harbour

پارک

park

نیمکت

bench

پل

bridge

پله

stairs

مترو

underground

تونل

tunnel

ایستگاه اتوبوس

bus stop

میخانه

bar

رستوران

restaurant

صندوق پست

postbox

تابلوی خیابان

street sign

دستگاه پارکومتر

parking meter

باغ وحش

zoo

استخر شنای عمومی

swimming pool

مسجد

mosque

مزرعه

farm

آلودگی محیط زیست

pollution

قبرستان

graveyard

کلیسا

church

زمین بازی

playground

معبد

temple

چشم انداز

landscape

برگ
leaf

تابلوی راهنمای مسیر
signpost

راه
way

چمنزار
meadow

سنگ
stone

درخت
tree

راه نورد
hiker

رودخانه
river

چمن
grass

گل
flower

دره
....
valley

تپه
....
hill

دریاچه
....
lake

جنگل
....
forest

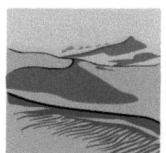

بیابان
....
desert

کوه آتشفشان
....
volcano

قلعه
....
castle

رنگین کمان
....
rainbow

قارچ
....
mushroom

درخت نخل
....
palm tree

پشه
....
mosquito

مگس
....
fly

مورچه
....
ant

زنبور
....
bee

عنکبوت
....
spider

سوسک
....
beetle

قورباغه
....
frog

سنجاب
....
squirrel

جوجه تیغی
....
hedgehog

خرگوش صحرایی
....
hare

جغد
....
owl

پرنده
....
bird

قو
....
swan

گراز
....
boar

گوزن نر
....
deer

گوزن شمالی
....
moose

سد آب
....
dam

توربین بادی
....
wind turbine

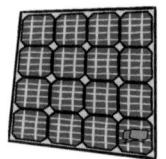

صفحه ی خورشیدی
....
solar panel

آب و هوا
....
climate

رستوران

restaurant

پیشخدمت رستوران
waiter
منوی غذا
menu
صندلی
chair
سوپ
soup
پیتزا
pizza
سرویس کارد و قاشق و چنگال
cutlery
رومیزی
tablecloth

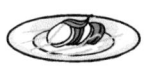

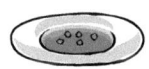

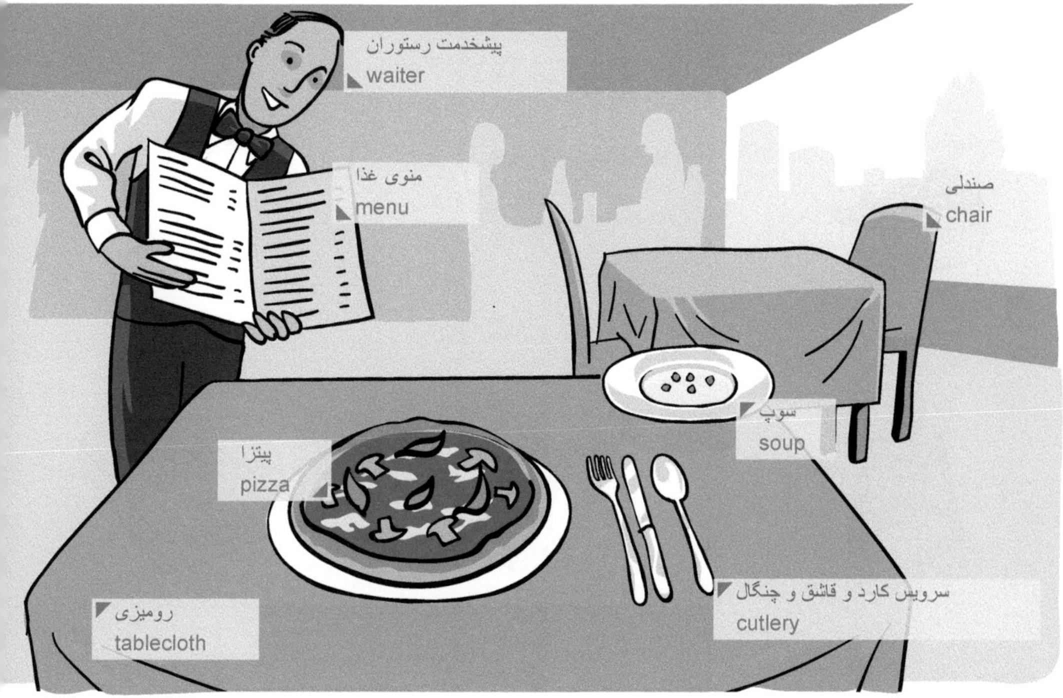

پیش‌غذا

starter

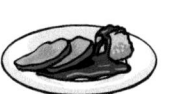

غذای اصلی

main course

دسر

dessert

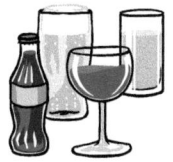

نوشیدنی ها

drinks

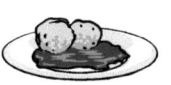

غذا

food

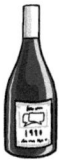

بطری

bottle

فست فود

fast food

اغذیه خیابانی

street food

قوری

teapot

قندان

sugar bowl

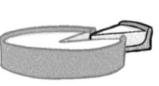

پُرس غذا

portion

دستگاه اسپرسو

espresso machine

صندلی پایه بلند غذاخوری بچه

high chair

صورتحساب

bill

سینی

tray

چاقو

knife

چنگال

fork

قاشق

spoon

قاشق چایخوری

teaspoon

دستمال سفره

serviette

لیوان

glass

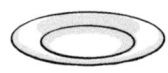

بشقاب
....
plate

بشقاب سوپخوری
....
soup plate

نعلبکی
....
saucer

سس
....
sauce

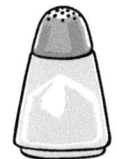

نمکدان
....
salt pot

فلفل ساب
....
pepper mill

سرکه
....
vinegar

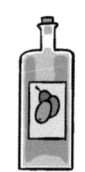

روغن خوراکی
....
oil

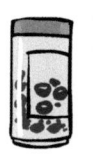

ادویه جات
....
spices

سس کچاپ
....
ketchup

سس خردل
....
mustard

سس مایونز
....
mayonnaise

سوپرمارکت

supermarket

پیشنهاد ویژه
special offer
FOR
مشتری
customer
لبنیات
dairy
میوه جات
fruit
چرخ دستی خرید
trolley

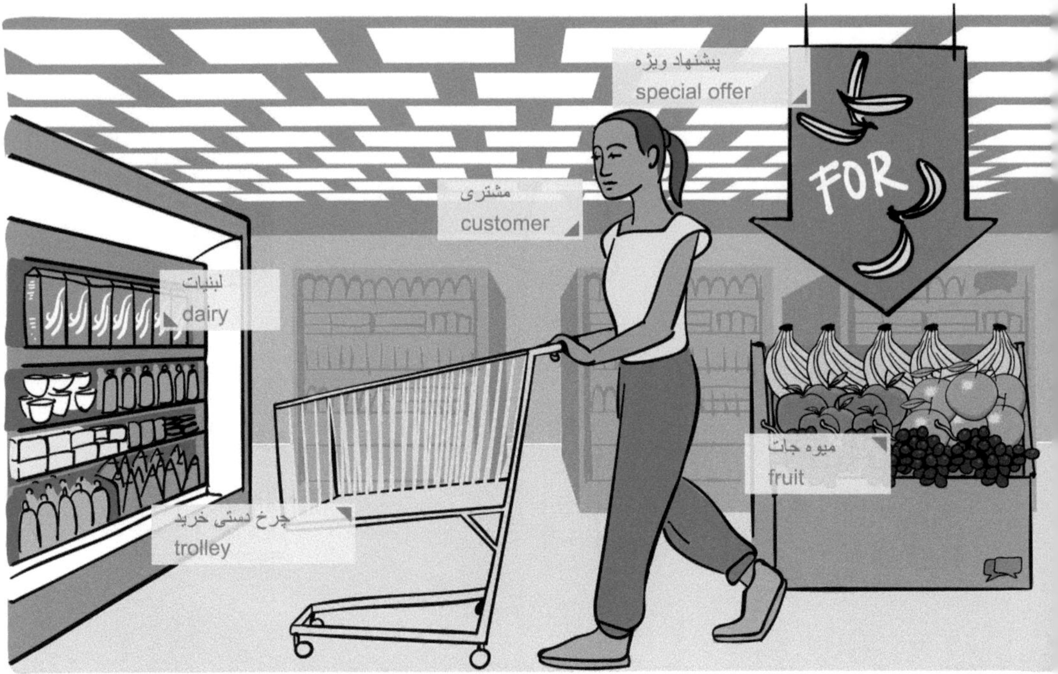

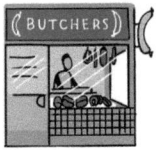

BUTCHERS

قصابی

butcher´s

BAKERY

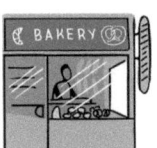

نانوایی

baker´s

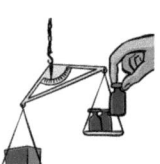

وزن کردن

weigh

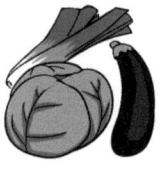

سبزیجات

vegetables

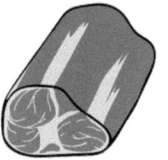

گوشت

meat

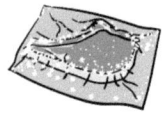

غذای منجمد

frozen food

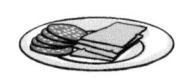

مخلوطی از انواع کالباس یا پنیر که
ورقه ای بریده شده باشند
....
cold meat

غذای کنسروی
....
tinned food

پودر لباسشویی
....
washing powder

شیرینی جات
....
sweets

لوازم خانگی
....
household products

ماده شوینده و پاک کننده
....
cleaning products

فروشنده
....
salesperson

صندوق پرداخت
....
till

صندوقدار
....
cashier

لیست خرید
....
shopping list

ساعات کار
....
opening hours

کیف پول
....
wallet

کارت اعتباری
....
credit card

کیف
....
bag

کیسه ی پلاستیکی
....
plastic bag

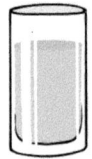

آب
....
water

آبمیوه
....
juice

شیر
....
milk

نوشابه کوکاکولا
....
coke

شراب
....
wine

آبجو
....
beer

الکل
....
alcohol

کاکائو
....
cocoa

چای
....
tea

قهوه
....
coffee

قهوه اسپرسو
....
espresso

کاپوچینو
....
cappuccino

موز

banana

سیب

apple

پرتقال

orange

انواع هندوانه و خربزه

melon

لیمو

lemon

هویج

carrot

سیر

garlic

نی بامبو

bamboo

پیاز

onion

قارچ

mushroom

آجیل

nuts

ماکارونی

noodles

اسپاگتی

spaghetti

برنج

rice

سالاد

salad

سیب زمینی سرخ کرده

chips

سیب زمینی سرخ شده

fried potatoes

پیتزا

pizza

همبرگر

hamburger

ساندویچ

sandwich

شنیتسل

cutlet

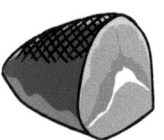

ژامبون خوک

ham

سالامی

salami

سوسیس

sausage

مرغ

chicken

نوعی گوشت سرخ شده

roast

ماهی

fish

جوی پرک شده
....
porridge oats

نوعی صبحانه مخلوطی از برگه ذرت و
میوه های خشک شده و خشکبار که
معمولا با شیر خورده می شود
muesli

کورن‌فلکس
....
cornflakes

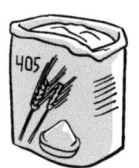

آرد
....
flour

کرواسان
....
croissant

نان بروتشن
....
bread roll

نان
....
bread

نان تست
....
toast

بیسکویت
....
biscuits

کره
....
butter

کشک
....
curd

کیک
....
cake

تخم مرغ
....
egg

تخم مرغ نیمرو
....
fried egg

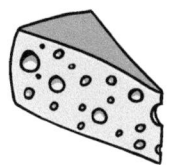

پنیر
....
cheese

بستنی

ice cream

شکر

sugar

عسل

honey

مربا

jam

کرم شکلاتی بادامی

chocolate spread

ادویه کاری

curry

مزرعه

farm

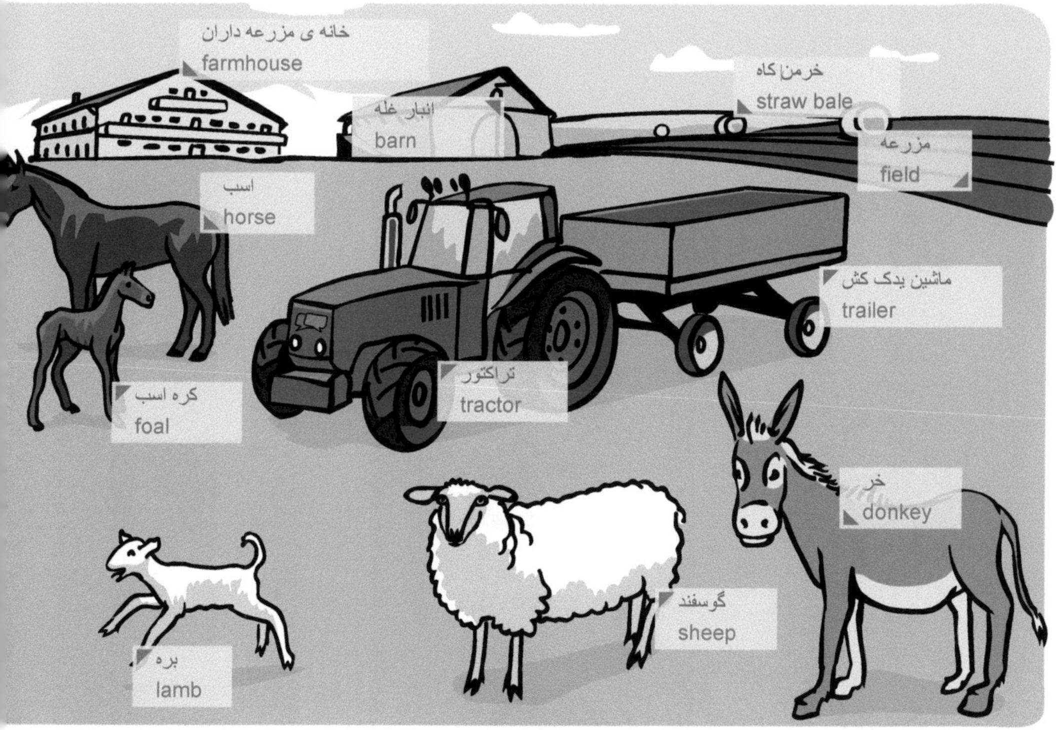

خانه ی مزرعه داران
farmhouse
انبار غله
barn
خرمن کاه
straw bale
مزرعه
field
اسب
horse
ماشین یدک کش
trailer
تراکتور
tractor
کره اسب
foal
خر
donkey
گوسفند
sheep
بره
lamb

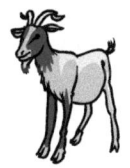

بز

goat

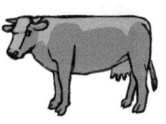

گاو ماده

cow

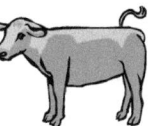

گوساله

calf

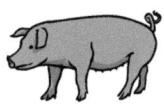

خوک

pig

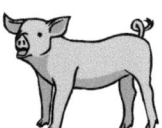

بچه خوک

piglet

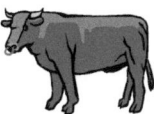

گاو نر

bull

غاز
....
goose

اردک
....
duck

جوجه
....
chick

مرغ
....
hen

خروس
....
cock

موش صحرایی
....
rat

گربه
....
cat

موش
....
mouse

گاو نر اخته
....
ox

سگ
....
dog

لانه ی سگ
....
doghouse

شلنگ باغبانی
....
garden hose

آبپاش
....
watering can

داس دسته بلند
....
scythe

گاوآهن
....
plough

مزرعه - farm

داس
....
sickle

کج بیل
....
hoe

چنگک باغبانی
....
pitchfork

تبر
....
axe

فرقون
....
wheelbarrow

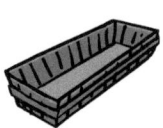

آبشخور
....
trough

بطری نگهداری شیر
....
milk can

کیسه
....
sack

حصار
....
fence

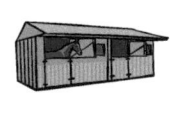

اصطبل
....
stable

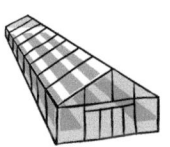

گلخانه
....
greenhouse

خاک
....
soil

بذر
....
seed

کود
....
fertilizer

ماشین کمباین
....
combine harvester

برداشت کردن محصول
....
harvest

محصول
....
harvest

تمیس
....
yams

گندم
....
wheat

سویا
....
soy

سیب زمینی
....
potato

ذرت
....
corn

کلزا
....
rapeseed

درخت میوه
....
fruit tree

گیاه مانیوک
....
cassava

غلات
....
cereals

خانه
house

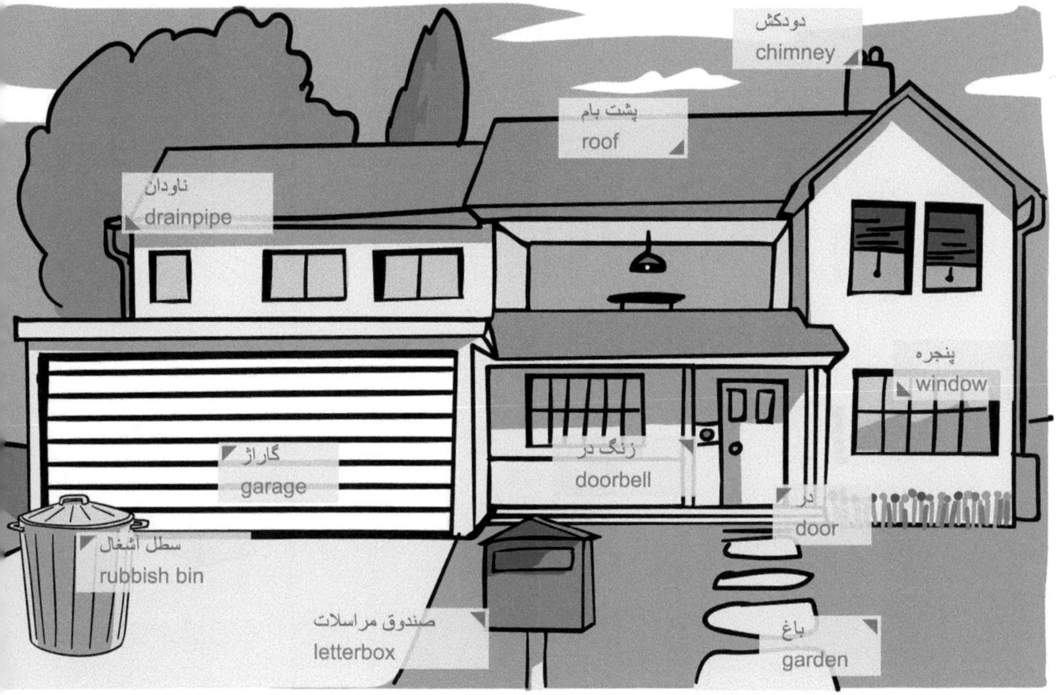

دودکش
chimney
پشت بام
roof
ناودان
drainpipe
پنجره
window
گاراژ
garage
زنگ در
doorbell
در
door
سطل آشغال
rubbish bin
صندوق مراسلات
letterbox
باغ
garden

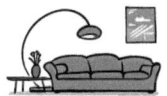

اتاق نشیمن
....
living room

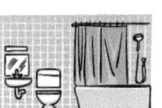

حمام
....
bathroom

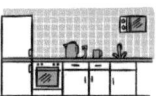

آشپزخانه
....
kitchen

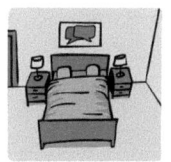

اتاق خواب
....
bedroom

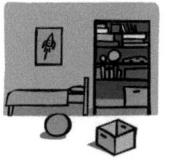

اتاق بچه
....
child's room

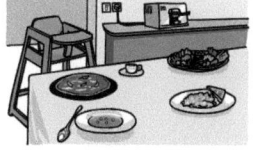

ناهارخوری
....
dining room

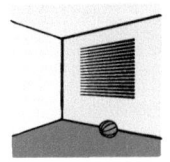

کف زمین

floor

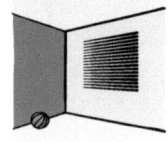

دیوار

wall

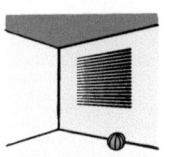

سقف

ceiling

زیرزمین

cellar

سونا

sauna

بالکن

balcony

تراس

terrace

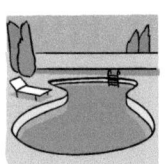

استخر

pool

ماشین چمن‌زنی

lawn mower

ملافه

sheet

روتختی

bedspread

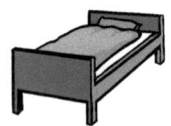

تخت خواب

bed

جارو

broom

سطل

bucket

سویچ یا کلید

switch

اتاق نشیمن

living room

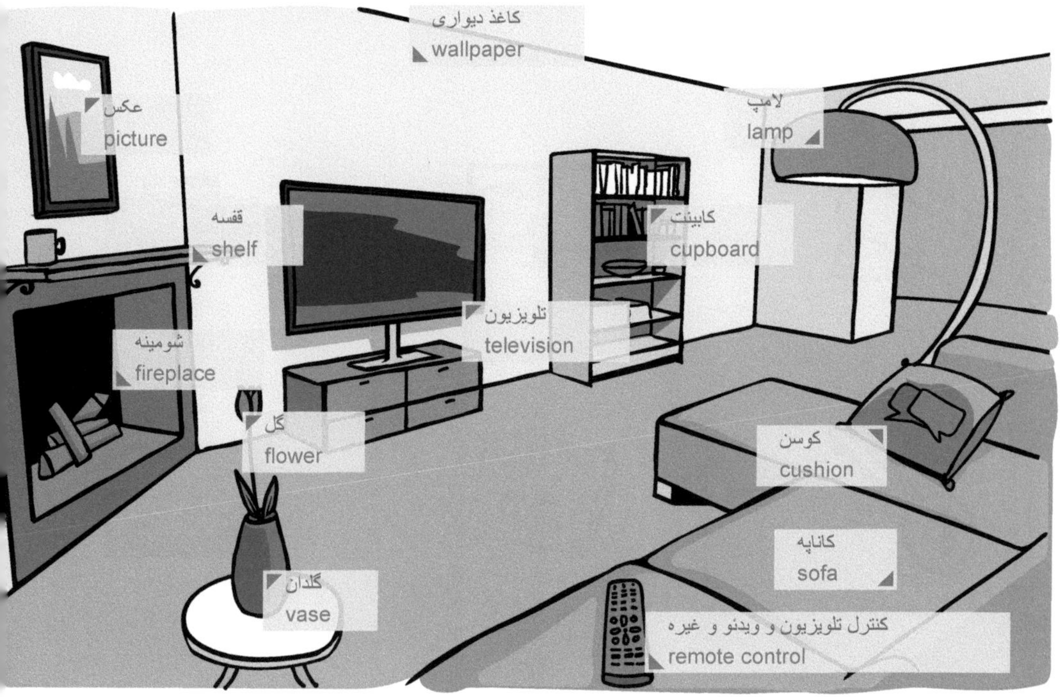

کاغذ دیواری
wallpaper
عکس
picture
لامپ
lamp
قفسه
shelf
کابینت
cupboard
تلویزیون
television
شومینه
fireplace
گل
flower
کوسن
cushion
کاناپه
sofa
گلدان
vase
کنترل تلویزیون و ویدئو و غیره
remote control

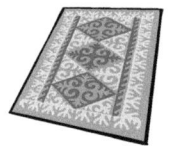

فرش
carpet

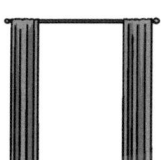

پرده
curtain

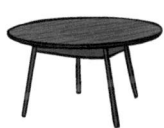

میز
table

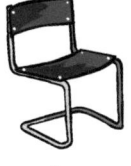

صندلی
chair

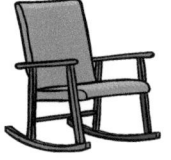

صندلی گهواره ایی
rocking chair

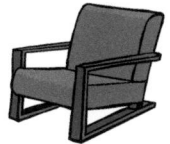

صندلی راحتی
armchair

كتاب

book

لحاف

blanket

دكوراسيون

decoration

هيزم

firewood

فيلم

film

دستگاه ضبط صوت

hi-fi equipment

كليد

key

روزنامه

newspaper

تابلو نقاشى

painting

پوستر

poster

راديو

radio

دفترچه يادداشت

notepad

جاروبرقى

hoover

كاكتوس

cactus

شمع

candle

آشپزخانه
kitchen

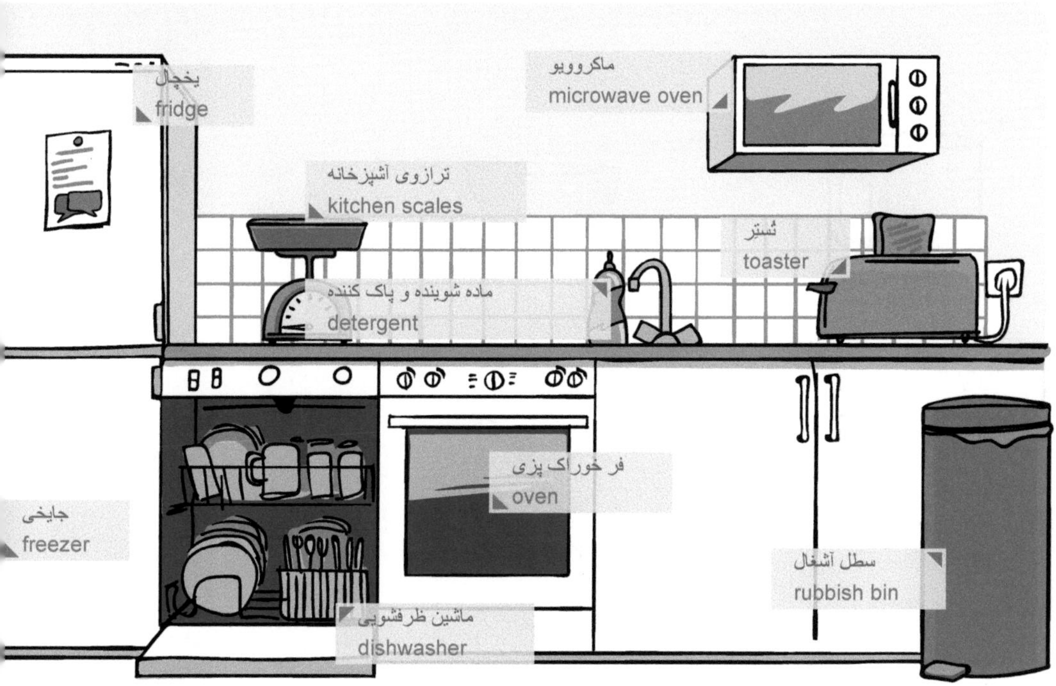
یخچال
fridge
ماکروویو
microwave oven
ترازوی آشپزخانه
kitchen scales
تُستر
toaster
ماده شوینده و پاک کننده
detergent
فر خوراک پزی
oven
جایخی
freezer
سطل آشغال
rubbish bin
ماشین ظرفشویی
dishwasher

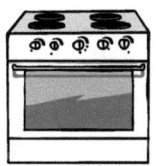

اجاق گاز
....
cooker

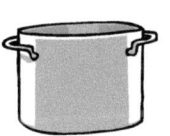

قابلمه
....
pot

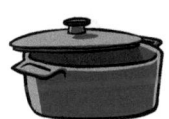

قابلمه چدنی
....
cast-iron pot

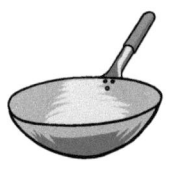

ماهی تابه گود
....
wok / kadai

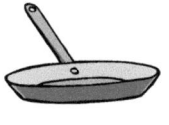

ماهی تابه
....
pan

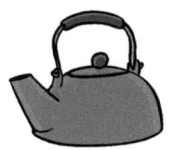

کتری
....
kettle

بخارپز

steamer

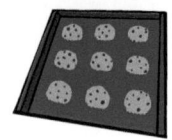

سینی فر

baking tray

ظرف چینی آشپزخانه

crockery

لیوان

mug

کاسه

bowl

چاپستیک

chopsticks

ملاقه

ladle

کفگیر

spatula

همزن

whisk

آبکش

strainer

آبکش

sieve

رنده

grater

هاون

mortar

باربیکیو

barbecue

محل مخصوص افروختن آتش

open fire

تخته گوشت و سبزی

chopping board

وردنه

rolling pin

در بطری بازکن

corkscrew

قوطی

can

در قوطی بازکن

can opener

دستگیره پارچه ای

pot holder

سینک ظرفشویی

sink

برس گردگیری

brush

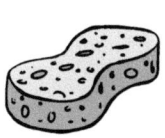

اسفنج

sponge

مخلوط کن

blender

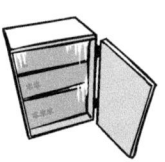

فریزر

deep freezer

شیشه شیر بچه

baby bottle

شیر آب

tap

حمام

bathroom

بخاری
heating
حوله
towel
دوش
shower
پرده ی حمام
shower curtain
حمام کف
bubble bath
وان حمام
bathtub
لیوان
glass
ماشین لباسشویی
washing machine
شیر آب
tap
کاشی
tiles
لگن دستشویی کودکان
potty
سینک ظرفشویی
sink

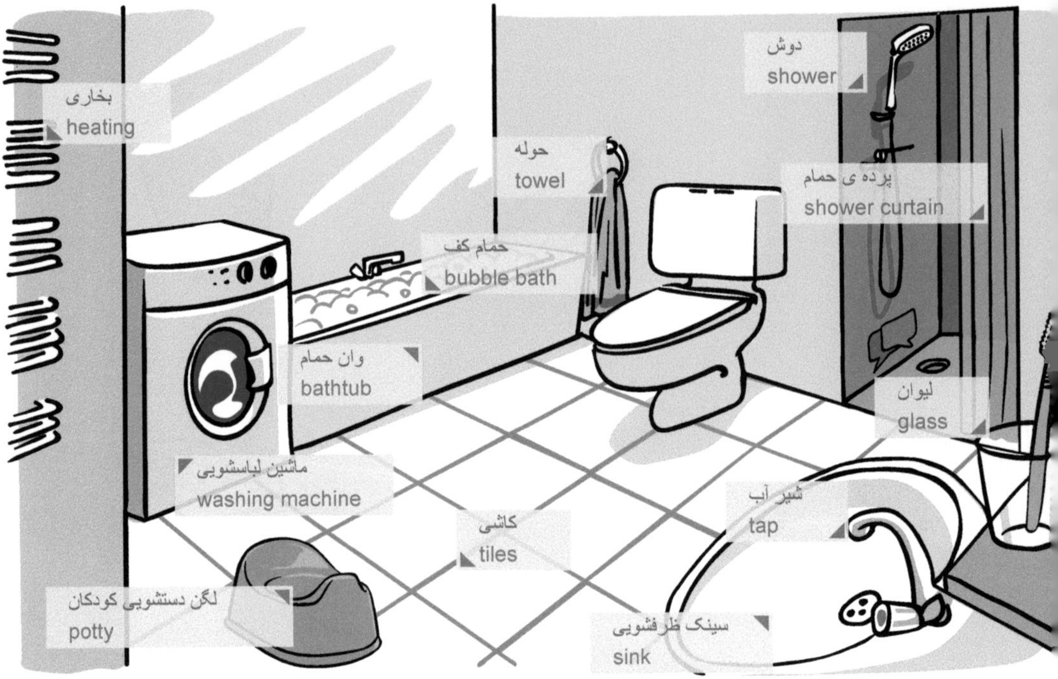

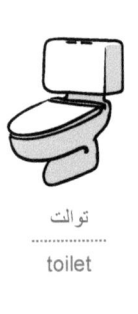

توالت
toilet

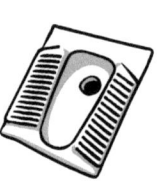

توالت ایرانی
squat toilet

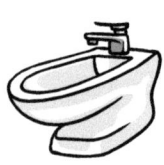

کاسه توالت
bidet

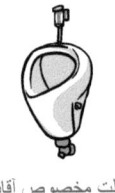

توالت مخصوص آقایان
urinal

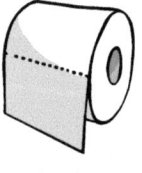

دستمال توالت
toilet paper

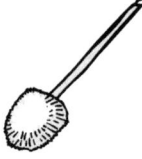

فرچه توالت
toilet brush

مسواک

toothbrush

خمیردندان

toothpaste

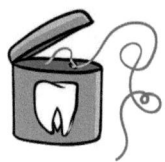

نخ دندان

dental floss

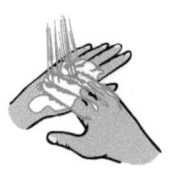

شستن

wash

دوش آب تلفنی

handheld shower

شلنگ توالت

douche

لگن روشویی

basin

برس شست و شوی پشت

back brush

صابون

soap

شامپو بدن

shower gel

شامپو

shampoo

لیف حمام

flannel

راه آب

drain

کرم

cream

اسپری دئودورانت

deodorant

آیینه

mirror

آیینه ی کوچک دستی

hand mirror

تیغ ریش تراشی

razor

کف ریش تراشی

shaving foam

أفترشیو

aftershave

شانه ی سر

comb

برس

brush

سشوار

hair dryer

اسپری مو

hairspray

آرایش

makeup

رژلب

lipstick

لاک ناخن

nail varnish

پنبه

cotton wool

قیچی ناخن

nail scissors

عطر

perfume

کیف لوازم آرایشی و بهداشتی

washbag

چهارپایه

stool

ترازو

weighing scale

حوله ی پالتویی

bathrobe

دستکش ظرفشویی

rubber gloves

تامپون

tampon

نوار بهداشتی

sanitary towel

توالت سیار

chemical toilet

اتاق بچه
child's room

ساعت زنگدار
alarm clock
نوعی عروسک نرم به شکل حیوانات
cuddly toy
ماشین اسباب بازی
toy car
جغجغه
rattle
خانه ی عروسکی
doll's house
کادو
present

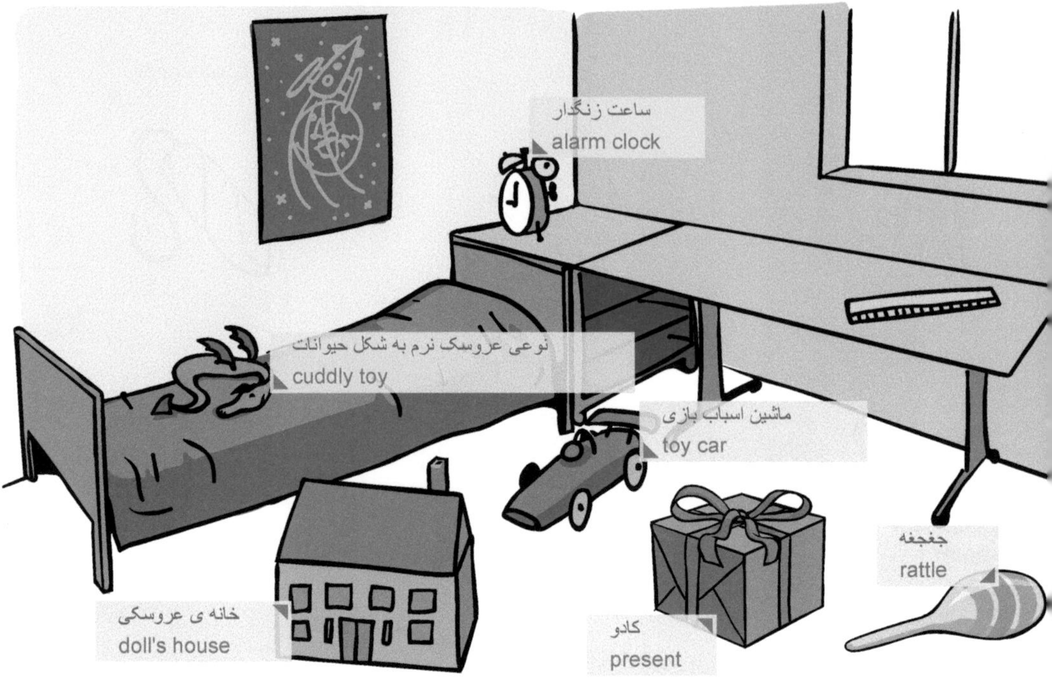

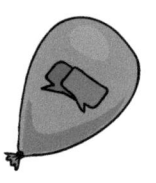

بادکنک

balloon

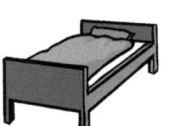

تخت خواب

bed

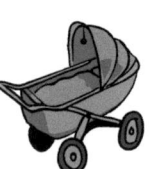

کالسکه بچه

pram

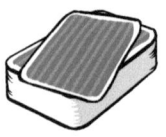

بازی ورق

deck of cards

پازل

jigsaw

SUPER
MEGA

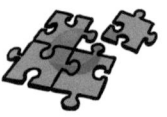

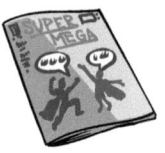

داستان مصور

comic

اسباب بازی لگو

lego bricks

خانه سازی

building blocks

عروسک شخصیت های فیلم و کارتون

action figure

لباس نوزاد

babygrow

فریزبی

frisbee

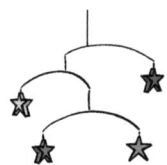

نوعی اسباب بازی که روی تخت نوزاد
یا کودک نصب می شود

mobile

بازی روی صفحه

board game

تاس

dice

قطار اسباب بازی

model train set

پستانک

dummy

مهمانی

party

کتاب مصور

picture book

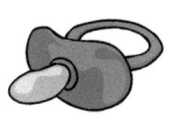

توپ

ball

عروسک

doll

بازی کردن

play

جعبه شنی مخصوص بازی کودکان

sandpit

تاب

swing

اسباب بازی

toys

کنسول بازی های کامپیوتری

video game console

سه چرخه

tricycle

خرس عروسکی

teddy bear

کمد لباس

wardrobe

لباس

clothing

جوراب

socks

جوراب زنانه ساق بلند

stockings

جوراب شلواری

tights

شال
scarf

چتر
umbrella

تی شرت
t-shirt

کمربند
belt

پوتین
boots

دمپایی
slippers

کفش ورزشی کتانی
trainers

صندل
....
sandals

کفش
....
shoes

چکمه پلاستیکی
....
rubber boots

شرت
....
underpants

سوتین
....
bra

جلیقه
....
vest

لباس - clothing

بادی

body

شلوار

trousers

جین

jeans

دامن

skirt

بلوز

blouse

پیراهن

shirt

پولیور

pullover

سویی شرت

hoodie

نوعی کت

blazer

ژاکت

jacket

کت بلند

coat

بارانی

raincoat

لباس نمایش

costume

لباس

dress

لباس عروس

wedding dress

کت و شلوار

suit

لباس خواب زنانه

nightgown

پیژامه

pyjamas

ساری

sari

روسری

headscarf

عمامه

turban

برقع

burqa

قبا

kaftan

عبا

abaya

لباس شنا

swimsuit

شرت شنا

trunks

شلوارک

shorts

لباس ورزشی

tracksuit

پیشبند

apron

دستکش

gloves

دکمه

button

عینک

glasses

دستبند

bracelet

گردنبند

necklace

انگشتر

ring

گوشواره

earring

کلاه لبه دار

cap

چوب لباسی

coat hanger

کلاه

hat

کراوات

tie

زیپ

zip

کلاه ایمنی

helmet

بند شلوار

braces

لباس مدرسه

school uniform

لباس فرم

uniform

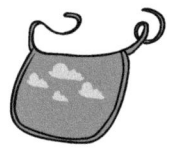

پیش بند بچه

bib

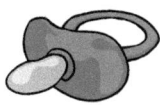

پستانک

dummy

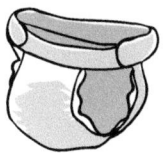

پوشک بچه

nappy

اداره

office

سرور
server
کمد نگهداری پرونده
filing cabinet
چاپگر
printer
کاغذ
paper
مانیتور
monitor
ماوس
mouse
میز تحریر
desk
زونکن
folder
صفحه کلید
keyboard
سبد کاغذ باطله
waste-paper basket
کامپیوتر
computer
صندلی
chair

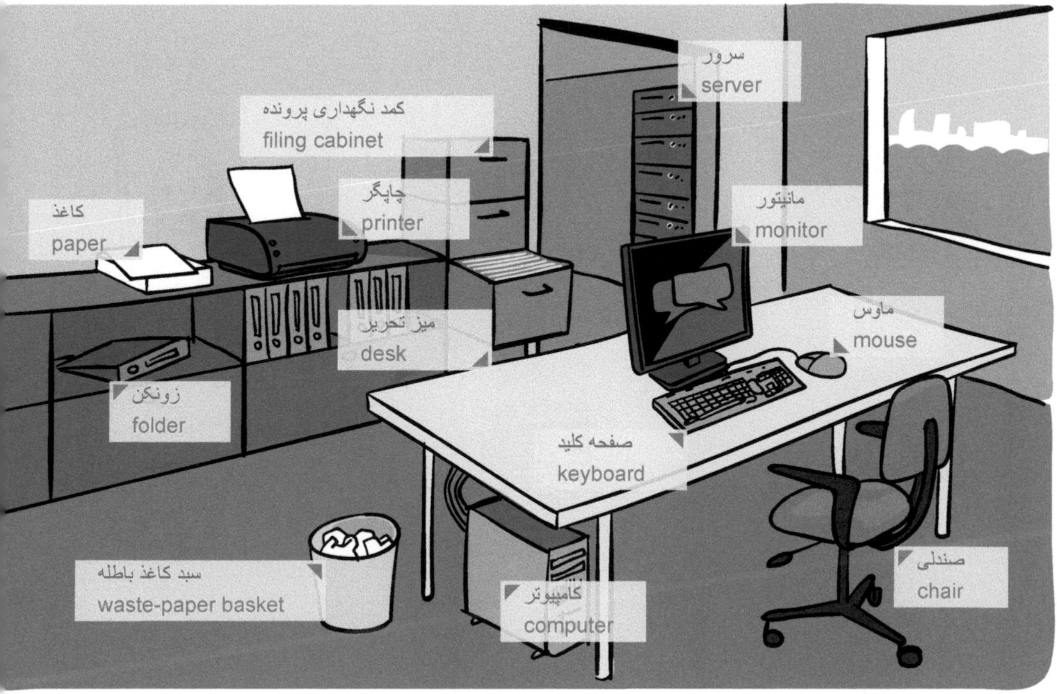

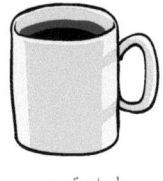

لیوان قهوه

coffee mug

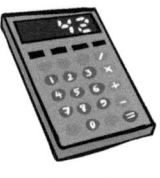

ماشین حساب

calculator

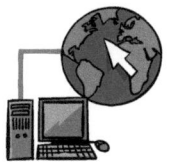

اینترنت

internet

پ تاپ

laptop

نامه

letter

پیغام

message

تلفن همراه

mobile

شبکه ی ارتباطی

network

دستگاه فتوکپی

photocopier

نرم افزار

software

تلفن

telephone

پریز

plug socket

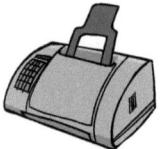

دستگاه فاکس

fax machine

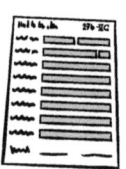

فرم

form

مدرک

document

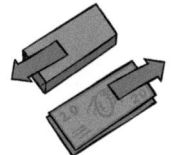

خریدن

buy

پرداخت کردن

pay

تجارت کردن

trade

پول

money

دلار

dollar

یورو

euro

ین

yen

روبل

rouble

فرانک سوئیس

Swiss franc

یوان رنمینبی

renminbi yuan

روپیه

rupee

دستگاه خودپرداز

cashpoint

صرافی

bureau de change

طلا

gold

نقره

silver

نفت

oil

انرژی

energy

قیمت

price

قرارداد

contract

مالیات

tax

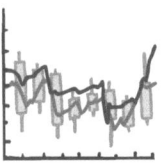

سهام سرمایه

stock

کار کردن

work

کارمند

employee

کارفرما

employer

کارخانه

factory

مغازه

shop

مشاغل
occupations

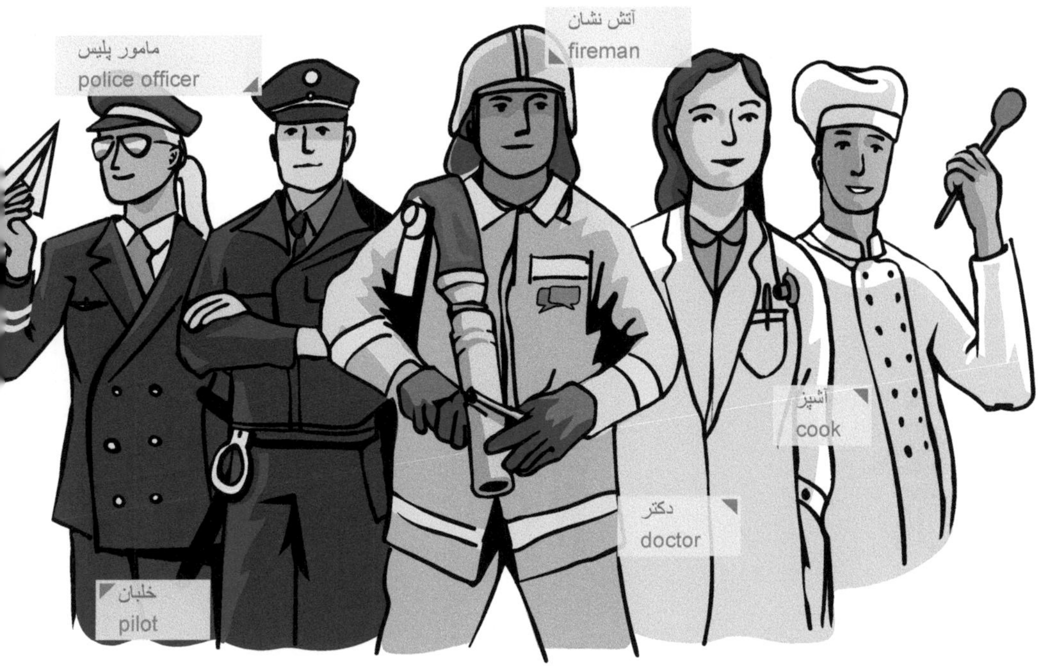

مامور پلیس
police officer
آتش نشان
fireman
آشپز
cook
دکتر
doctor
خلبان
pilot

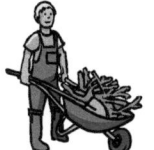

باغبان

gardener

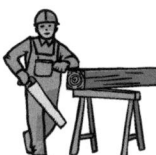

نجار

carpenter

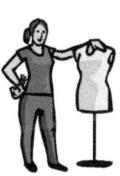

خیاط زنانه

seamstress

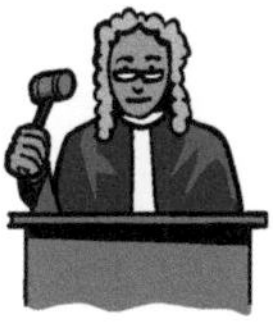

قاضی

judge

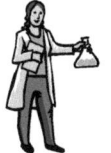

شیمیدان

chemist

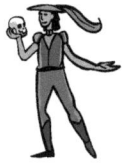

بازیگر

actor

راننده اتوبوس

bus driver

راننده تاکسی

taxi driver

ماهیگیر

fisherman

نظافتچی زن

cleaning lady

سقف ساز

roofer

پیشخدمت رستوران

waiter

شکارچی

hunter

نقاش

painter

نانوا

baker

برقکار

electrician

کارگر ساختمانی

builder

مهندس

engineer

قصاب

butcher

لوله کش

plumber

پستچی

postman

سرباز
....
soldier

معمار
....
architect

صندوقدار
....
cashier

گل فروش
....
florist

آرایشگر
....
hairdresser

مامور کنترل بلیط در قطار
....
conductor

مکانیک
....
mechanic

ناخدا
....
captain

دندانپزشک
....
dentist

دانشمند
....
scientist

عالم یهودی
....
rabbi

امام
....
imam

راهب
....
monk

کشیش
....
clergyman

ابزارآلات

tools

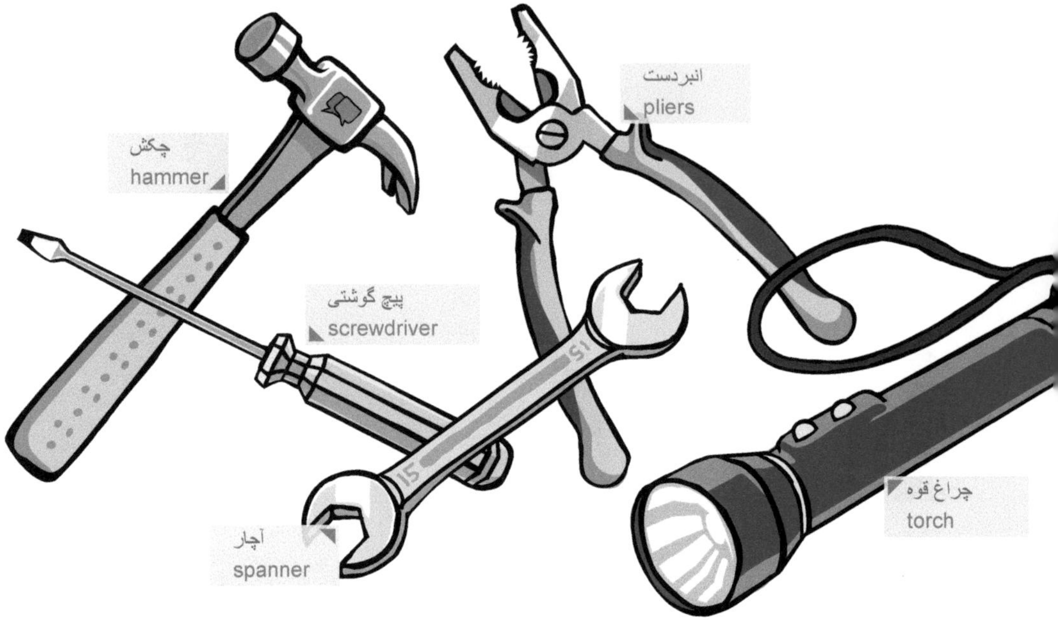

چکش
hammer
انبردست
pliers
پیچ گوشتی
screwdriver
آچار
spanner
چراغ قوه
torch

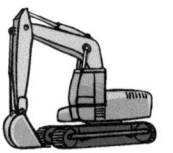

بیل مکانیکی

digger

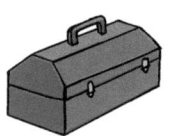

جعبه ابزار

toolbox

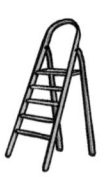

نردبان

ladder

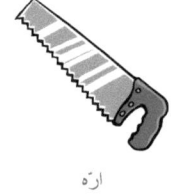

ارّه

saw

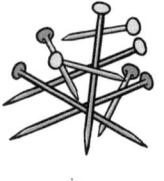

میخ

nails

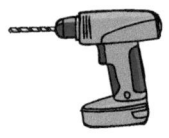

مته

drill

تعمیر کردن

repair

بیل

shovel

لعنتی!

Damn!

خاک انداز

dustpan

سطل رنگرزی

paint pot

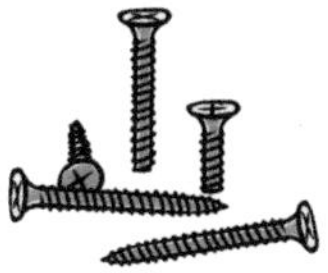

پیچ

screws

آلات موسیقی

musical instruments

بلندگو
loudspeaker

درامز
drum kit ◢

گیتار
guitar ◢

کنترباس
double bass

ترومپت
trumpet

پیانو
piano

ویولن
violin

گیتار بیس
bass

تیمپانی
timpani

طبل
drums

کیبورد الکتریک
keyboard

ساکسیفون
saxophone

فلوت
flute

میکروفون
microphone

باغ وحش

ZOO

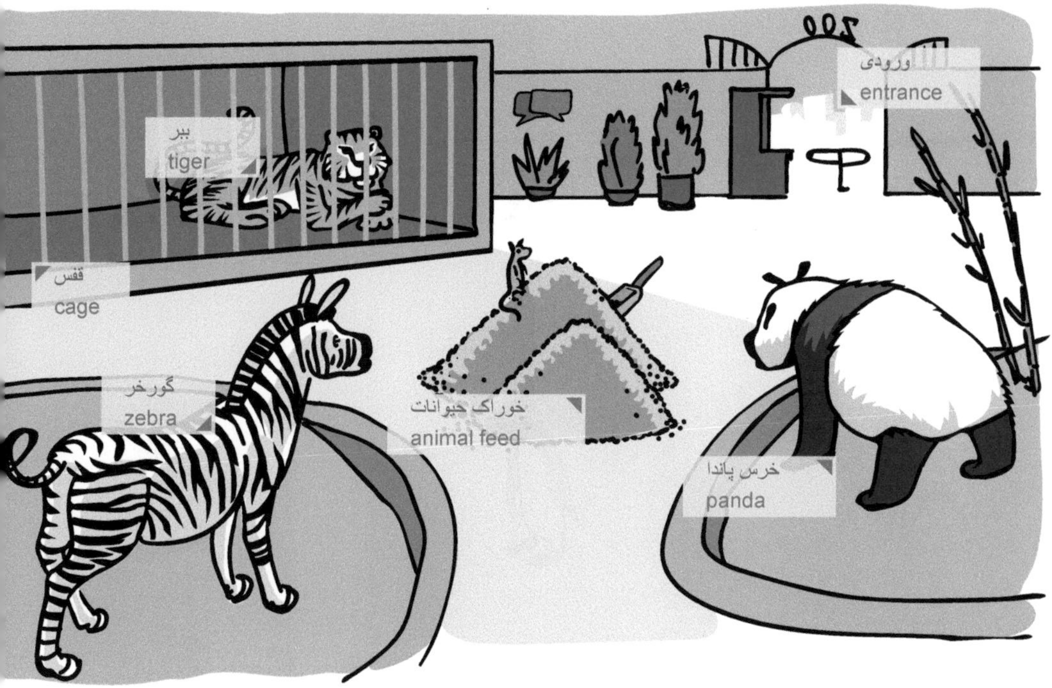

ورودی
entrance
ببر
tiger
قفس
cage
گورخر
zebra
خوراک حیوانات
animal feed
خرس پاندا
panda

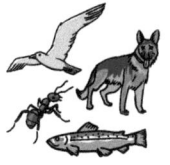

حیوانات

animals

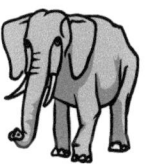

فیل

elephant

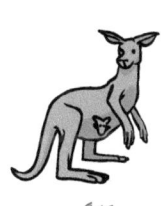

کانگورو

kangaroo

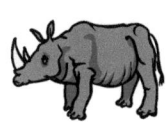

کرگدن

rhino

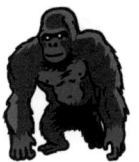

گوریل

gorilla

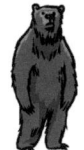

خرس

bear

شتر

camel

شترمرغ

ostrich

شیر

lion

میمون

monkey

فلامینگو

flamingo

طوطی

parrot

خرس قطبی

polar bear

پنگوئن

penguin

کوسه

shark

طاووس

peacock

مار

snake

تمساح

crocodile

نگهبان باغ وحش

zookeeper

خوک آبی

seal

پلنگ امریکایی

jaguar

اسب کوچک

pony

پلنگ

leopard

اسب آبی

hippo

زرافه

giraffe

عقاب

eagle

گراز

boar

ماهی

fish

لاک پشت

turtle

شیرماهی

walrus

روباه

fox

غزال

gazelle

فوتبال آمریکایی
American football

دوچرخه سواری
cycling

تنیس
tennis

بسکتبال
basketball

شنا
swimming

هاکی روی یخ
ice hockey

بوکس
boxing

فوتبال
football

بدمینتون
badminton

دوومیدانی
athletics

هندبال
handball

اسکی
skiing

پولو
polo

فعالیت ها

activities

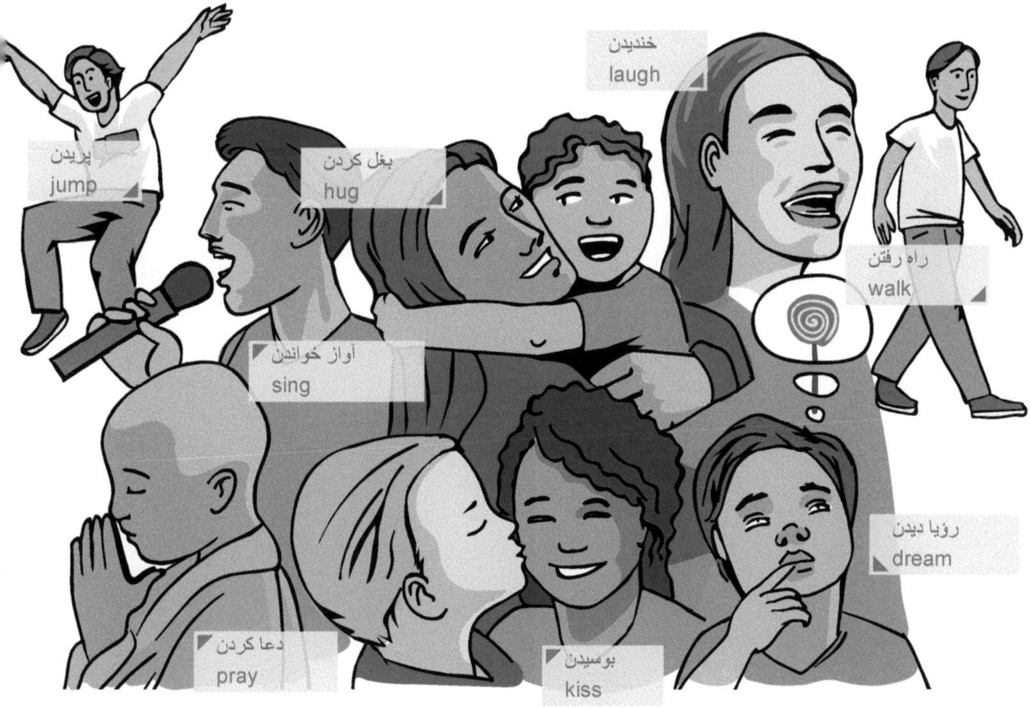

پریدن
jump
آواز خواندن
sing
بغل کردن
hug
خندیدن
laugh
راه رفتن
walk
رؤیا دیدن
dream
دعا کردن
pray
بوسیدن
kiss

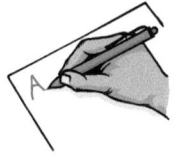

نوشتن

write

رسم کردن

draw

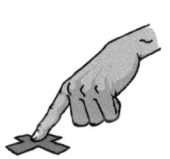

نشان دادن

show

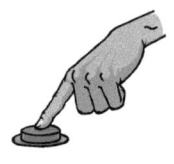

هل دادن

push

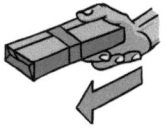

دادن

give

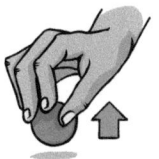

برداشتن

take

داشتن

have

انجام دادن

do

بودن

be

ایستادن

stand

دویدن

run

کشیدن

pull

پرتاب کردن

throw

افتادن

fall

دراز کشیدن

lie

منتظر بودن

wait

حمل کردن

carry

نشستن

sit

لباس پوشیدن

get dressed

خوابیدن

sleep

بیدار شدن

wake up

تماشا کردن

look at

گریه کردن

cry

نوازش کردن

stroke

شانه کردن

comb

حرف زدن

talk

فهمیدن

understand

پرسیدن

ask

شنیدن

listen

آشامیدن

drink

خوردن

eat

مرتب کردن

tidy up

عاشق بودن

love

پختن

cook

رانندگی کردن

drive

پرواز کردن

fly

قایقرانی کردن

sail

محاسبه کردن

calculate

خواندن

read

یاد گرفتن

learn

کار کردن

work

ازدواج کردن

marry

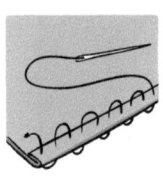

دوختن

sew

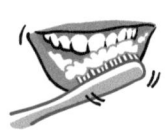

مسواک زدن

brush teeth

کشتن

kill

سیگار کشیدن

smoke

فرستادن

send

خانواده

family

مادربزرگ
grandmother
پدربزرگ
grandfather
پدر
father
مادر
mother
کودک
baby
فرزند دختر
daughter
فرزند پسر
son

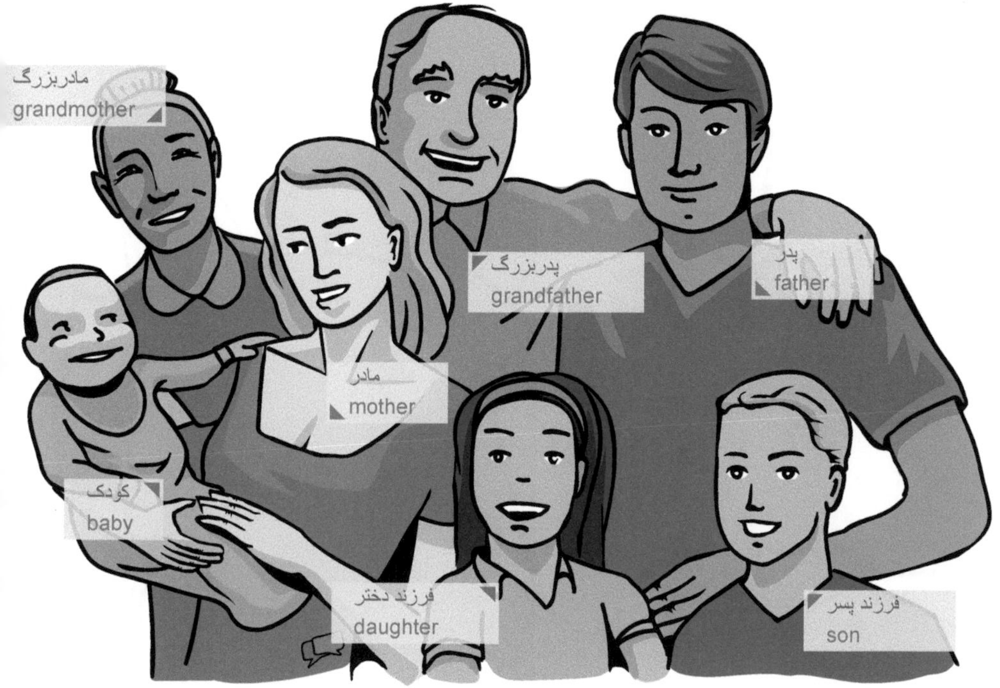

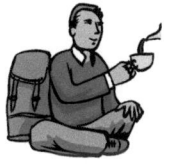

مهمان

guest

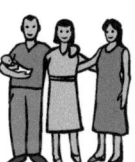

خاله، عمه

aunt

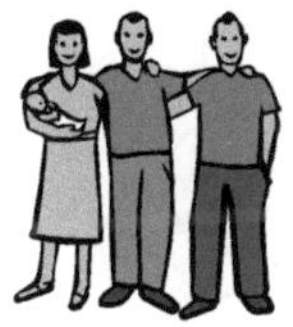

دایی، عمو

uncle

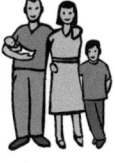

برادر

brother

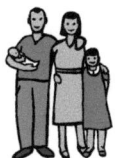

خواهر

sister

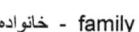

بدن

body

پیشانی
forehead
چشم
eye
شانه
shoulder
انگشت دست
finger
صورت
face
چانه
chin
دست
hand
ساق پا
leg
سینه
breast
بازو
arm

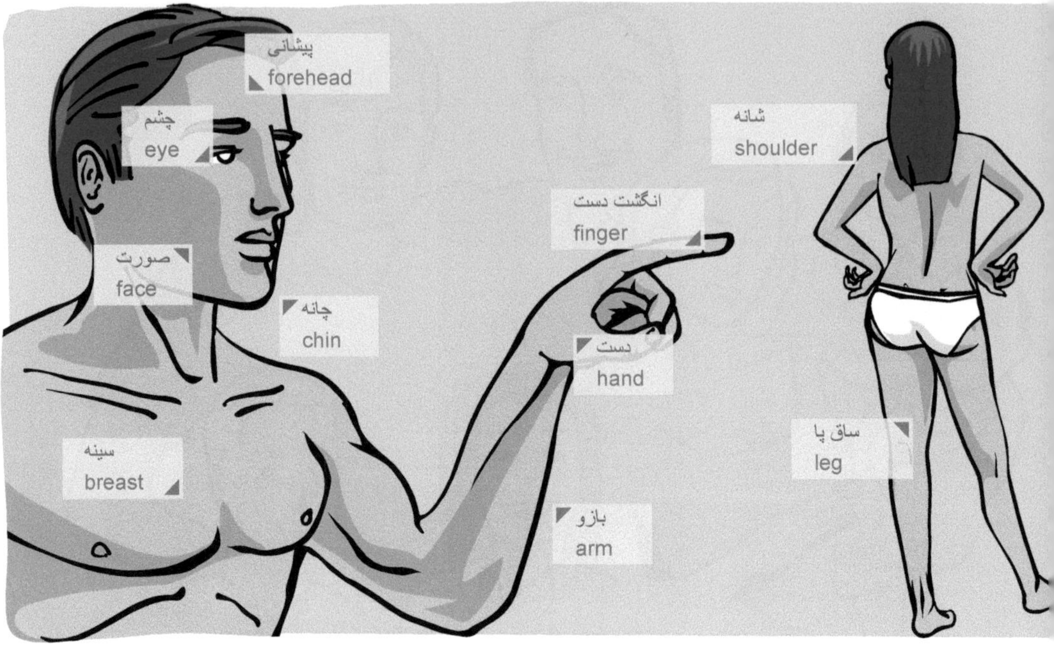

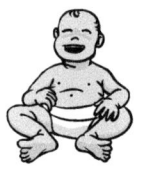

کودک

baby

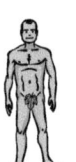

مرد

man

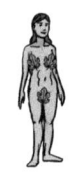

زن

woman

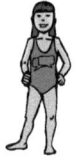

دختربچه

girl

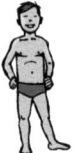

پسربچه

boy

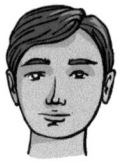

کله

head

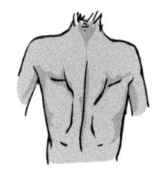

کمر
....
back

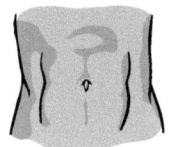

شکم
....
belly

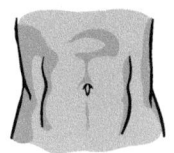

ناف
....
belly button

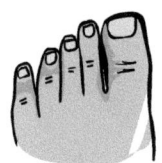

انگشت پا
....
toe

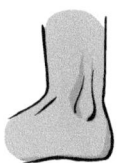

پاشنه
....
heel

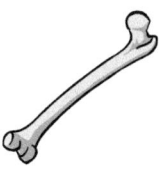

استخوان
....
bone

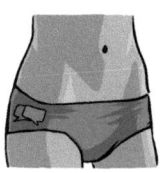

لگن
....
hip

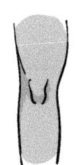

زانو
....
knee

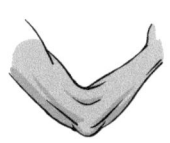

آرنج
....
elbow

بینی
....
nose

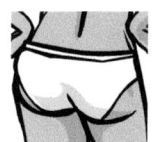

نشیمنگاه
....
bottom

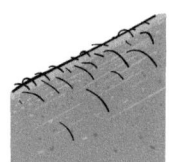

پوست
....
skin

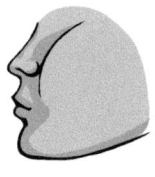

گونه
....
cheek

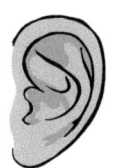

گوش
....
ear

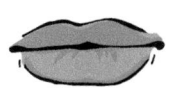

لب
....
lip

دهان

mouth

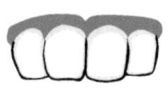

دندان

tooth

زبان

tongue

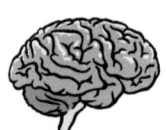

مغز

brain

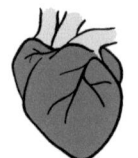

قلب

heart

عضله

muscle

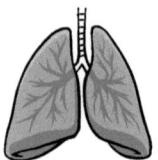

ریه

lung

کبد

liver

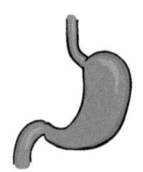

معده

stomach

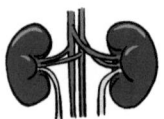

کلیه

kidneys

آمیزش جنسی

sex

کاندوم

condom

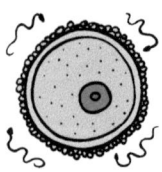

تخمک

ovum

اسپرم

semen

حاملگی

pregnancy

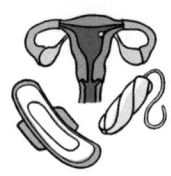

پریود
....
menstruation

واژن
....
vagina

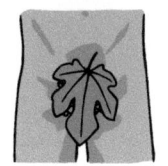

آلت تناسلی مرد
....
penis

ابرو
....
eyebrow

مو
....
hair

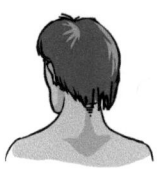

گردن
....
neck

بیمارستان

hospital

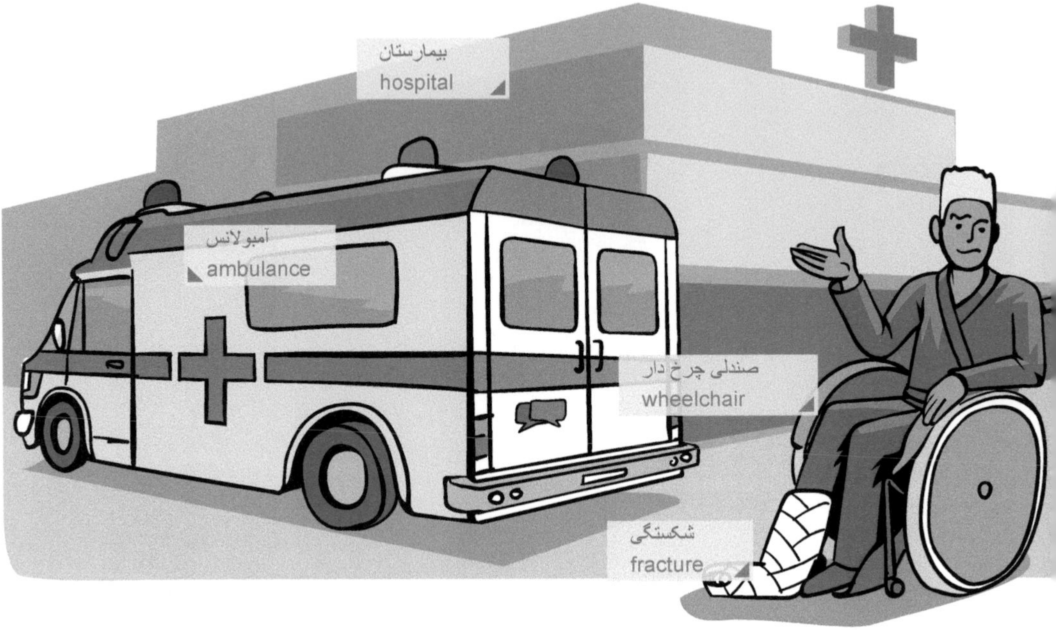

بیمارستان
hospital
آمبولانس
ambulance
صندلی چرخ دار
wheelchair
شکستگی
fracture

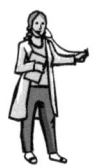

دکتر

doctor

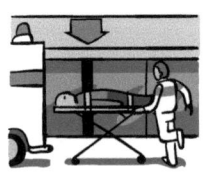

بخش اورژانس

emergency room

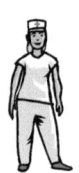

پرستار

nurse

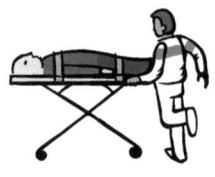

موقعیت اضطراری

emergency

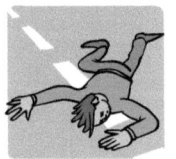

بی هوش

unconscious

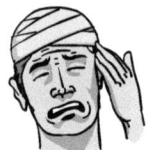

درد

pain

مصدومیت

injury

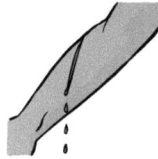

خونریزی

bleeding

سکته قلبی

heart attack

سکته مغزی

stroke

آلرژی

allergy

سرفه

cough

تب

fever

آنفولانزا

flu

اسهال

diarrhoea

سردرد

headache

سرطان

cancer

دیابت

diabetes

جراح

surgeon

چاقوی جراحی

scalpel

عمل جراحی

operation

سی تی اسکن

CT

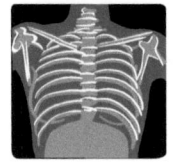

پرتونگاری

x-ray

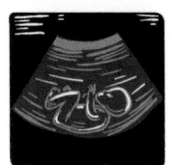

سونوگرافی

ultrasound

ماسک صورت

face mask

بیماری

disease

اتاق انتظار

waiting room

چوب زیر بغل

crutch

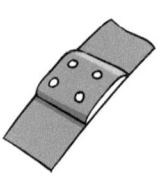

چسب زخم

plaster

پانسمان

bandage

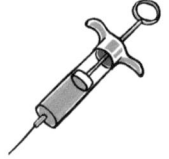

تزریق

injection

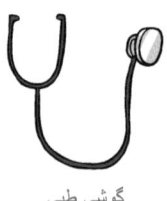

گوشی طبی

stethoscope

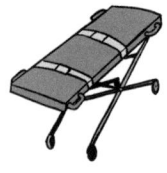

برانکار

stretcher

دماسنج

clinical thermometer

زایش

birth

اضافه وزن

overweight

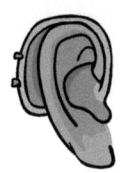

سمعک

hearing aid

ماده ضد غفونی کننده

disinfectant

عفونت

infection

ویروس

virus

اچ آی وی / ایدز

HIV / AIDS

دارو

medicine

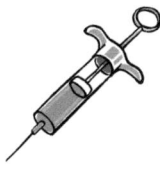

واکسیناسیون

vaccination

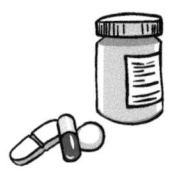

قرص

tablets

قرص ضد حاملگی

pill

تماس اظطراری

emergency call

دستگاه اندازه گیری فشارخون

blood pressure monitor

مریض / سالم

ill / healthy

کمک! \
Help!

آژیر خطر \
alarm

حمله \
assault

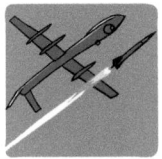

حمله ی فیزیکی \
attack

خطر \
danger

خروج اظطراری \
emergency exit

آتش \
Fire!

کپسول آتش‌نشانی \
fire extinguisher

تصادف \
accident

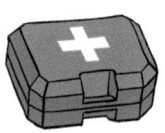

جعبه کمک های اولیه \
first-aid kit

درخواست کمک \
SOS

پلیس \
police

اروپا

Europe

آمریکای شمالی

North America

آمریکای جنوبی

South America

آفریقا

Africa

آسیا

Asia

استرالیا

Australia

اقیا نوس اطلس

Atlantic

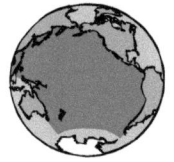

اقیانوس آرام

Pacific

اقیانوس هند

Indian Ocean

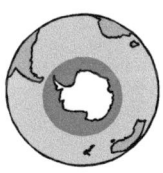

اقیا نوس اطلس جنوبی

Antarctic Ocean

اقیانوس منجمد شمالی

Arctic Ocean

قطب شمال

North Pole

قطب جنوب

South Pole

قاره قطب جنوب

Antarctica

کره زمین

Earth

سرزمین

land

دریا

sea

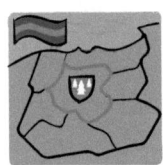

جزیره

island

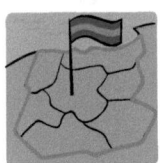

ملت

nation

کشور

state

صفحه ی ساعت

clock face

ساعت شمار

hour hand

دقیقه شمار

minute hand

ثانیه شمار

second hand

ساعت چند است؟

What time is it?

روز

day

زمان

time

اکنون

now

ساعت دیجیتال

digital watch

دقیقه

minute

ساعت

hour

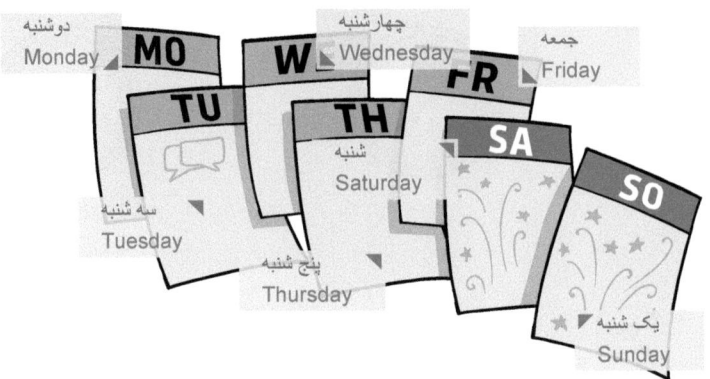

دوشنبه
Monday

چهارشنبه
Wednesday

جمعه
Friday

سه شنبه
Tuesday

شنبه
Saturday

پنج شنبه
Thursday

یک شنبه
Sunday

دیروز
....
yesterday

امروز
....
today

فردا
....
tomorrow

صبح
....
morning

ظهر
....
noon

غروب
....
evening

روزهای کاری
....
business days

آخر هفته
....
weekend

سال

year

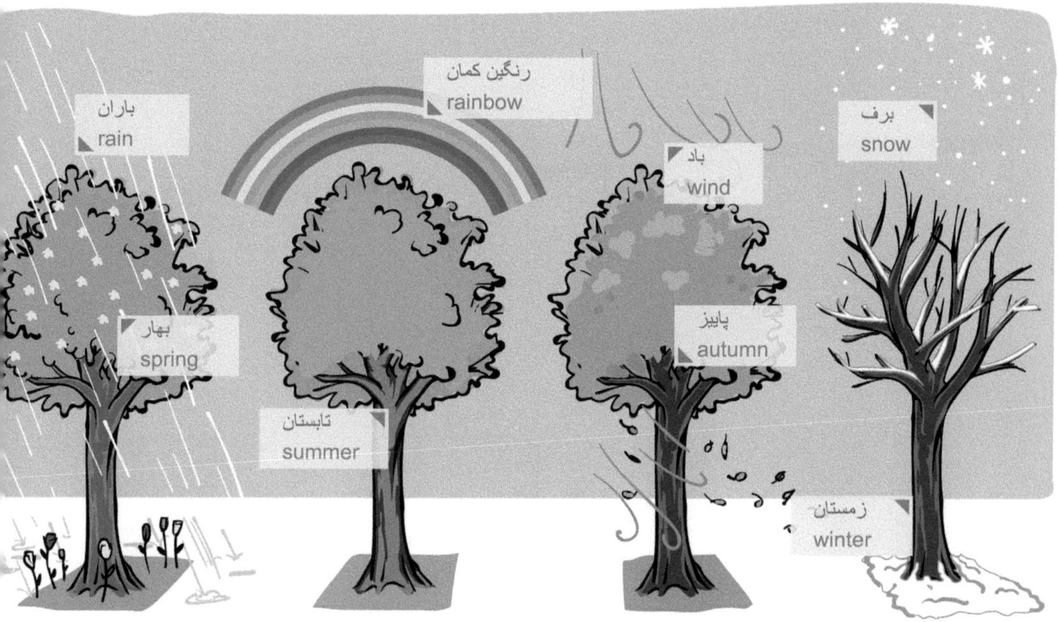

باران
rain
رنگین کمان
rainbow
باد
wind
برف
snow
بهار
spring
تابستان
summer
پاییز
autumn
زمستان
winter

4.APRIL 11°
5.APRIL 4°
6.APRIL 13°
7.APRIL 8°
8.APRIL 10°

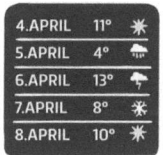

پیش‌بینی اوضاع جوی

weather forecast

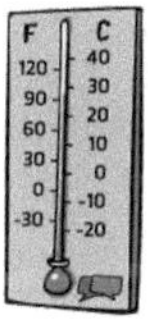

F C
120 40
90 30
60 20
30 10
0 0
-30 -10
-20

دماسنج

thermometer

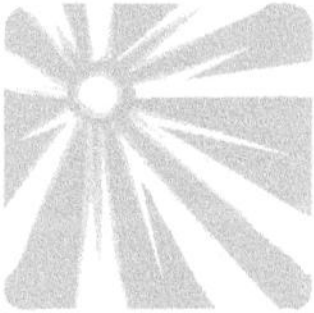

تابش آفتاب

sunshine

ابر

cloud

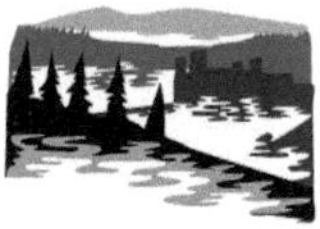

مِه

fog

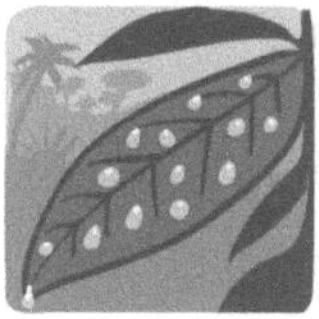

رطوبت هوا

humidity

صاعقه
....
lightning

آسمان غره
....
thunder

طوفان
....
storm

تگرگ
....
hail

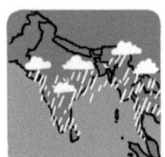

باد موسمی
....
monsoon

سیل
....
flood

یخ
....
ice

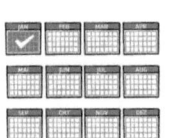

ژانویه
....
January

فوریه
....
February

مارس
....
March

آوریل
....
April

مه
....
May

ژوئن
....
June

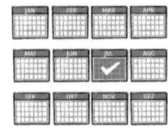

ژوئیه
....
July

آگوست
....
August

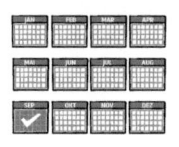

سپتامبر
....
September

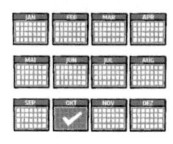

اکتبر
....
October

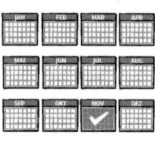

نوامبر
....
November

دسامبر
....
December

دایره
....
circle

مربع
....
square

مستطیل
....
rectangle

سه گوش
....
triangle

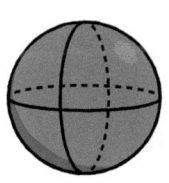

گره
....
sphere

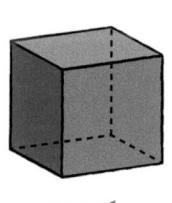

مکعب مربع
....
cube

سفید
white

زرد
yellow

نارنجی
orange

صورتی
pink

قرمز
red

بنفش
purple

آبی
blue

سبز
green

قهوه ای
brown

خاکستری
grey

سیاه
black

خیلی / کم

a lot / a little

خشمگین / آرام

angry / calm

زیبا / زشت

beautiful / ugly

شروع / پایان

beginning / end

بزرگ / کوچک

big / small

روشن / تیره

bright / dark

برادر / خواهر

brother / sister

تمیز / آلوده

clean / dirty

کامل / ناقص

complete / incomplete

روز / شب

day / night

مرده / زنده

dead / alive

پهن / باریک

wide / narrow

قابل خوردن / غیر قابل خوردن
....
edible / inedible

غضبناک / مهربان
....
evil / kind

هیجان زده / بی حوصله
....
excited / bored

چاق / لاغر
....
fat / thin

اولین / آخرین
....
first / last

دوست / دشمن
....
friend / enemy

پر / خالی
....
full / empty

سفت / نرم
....
hard / soft

سنگین / سبک
....
heavy / light

گرسنگی / تشنگی
....
hunger / thirst

مریض / سالم
....
ill / healthy

غیرقانونی / قانونی
....
illegal / legal

باهوش / خنگ
....
intelligent / stupid

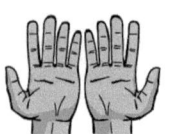

چپ / راست
....
left / right

نزدیک / دور
....
near / far

نو / استفاده شده

new / used

هیچ چیز / چیزی

nothing / something

پیر / جوان

old / young

روشن / خاموش

on / off

باز / بسته

open / closed

آهسته / بلند

quiet / loud

ثروتمند / فقیر

rich / poor

درست / غلط

right / wrong

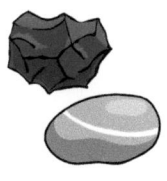

زبر / صاف

rough / smooth

غمگین / خوشحال

sad / happy

کوتاه / بلند

short / long

کند / تند

slow / fast

تر / خشک

wet / dry

گرم / خنک

warm / cool

جنگ / صلح

war / peace

numbers

0	**1**	**2**
صفر	یک	دو
zero	one	two
3	**4**	**5**
سه	چهار	پنج
three	four	five
6	**7**	**8**
شِش	هفت	هشت
six	seven	eight
9	**10**	**11**
نه	دَه	یازده
nine	ten	eleven

12

دوازده

twelve

13

سیزده

thirteen

14

چهارده

fourteen

15

پانزده

fifteen

16

شانزده

sixteen

17

هفده

seventeen

18

هجده

eighteen

19

نوزده

nineteen

20

بیست

twenty

100

صد

hundred

1.000

هزار

thousand

1.000.000

میلیون

million

انگلیسی

English

انگلیسی آمریکایی

American English

چینی ماندارین

Chinese Mandarin

هندی

Hindi

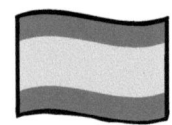

اسپانیایی

Spanish

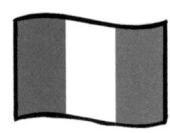

فرانسوی

French

عربی

Arabic

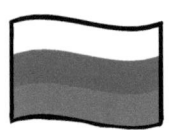

روسی

Russian

پرتغالی

Portuguese

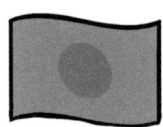

بنگالی

Bengali

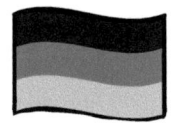

آلمانی

German

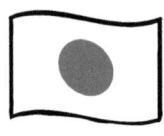

ژاپنی

Japanese

من

I

تو

you

او

he / she / it

ما

we

شما

you

آنها

they

چه کسی؟ کی؟

who?

چی؟

what?

چگونه؟

how?

کجا؟

where?

کی؟

when?

نام

name

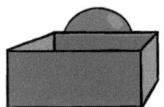

پشت

behind

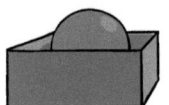

توی

in

جلو

in front of

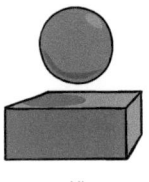

بالای

over

روی

on

زیر

under

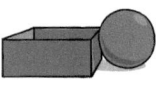

مجاور

beside

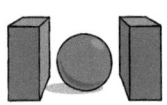

بین

between

مکان

place

ISBN   978-3-7511-9909-4

BABADADA dictionaries are visual language education: Simple learning takes center stage. In a BABADADA dictionary images and language merge into a unit that is easy to learn and remember. Each book contains over 1000 black-and-white illustrations. The goal is to learn the basics of a language much faster and with more fun than possible with a complicated text dictionary.

This book is based on the very successful online picture dictionary BABADADA.COM, which offers easy language entry for countless language combinations - Used by thousands of people and approved by well-known institutions.

BABADADA®

繁體中文（臺灣）

Traditional Chinese (Taiwan)

Tiếng Việt

Vietnamese

black-and-white

圖畫辭典

từ điển tranh minh họa